# UNDERSTANDING
# *Your 7*

# UNDERSTANDING
# *Your 7 year old*

## Elsie Osborne

of the

## TAVISTOCK CLINIC

*Series Editor: Elsie Osborne*

# ROSENDALE PRESS

First published in Great Britain in 1993,
reprinted 1999 by:
Rosendale Press Ltd
8 Ponsonby Place, London
London SW1P 4PT

Design by Pep Reiff
Production Edward Allhusen
Typeset by Ace Filmsetting Ltd
Printed in the United Kingdom by Cromwell Press

British Library Cataloguing in Publication Data
A catalogue record for this book is available from
The British Library

ISBN 1 872803 40 7

The Tavistock Clinic, London, was founded in 1920, in order to meet the needs of people whose lives had been disrupted by the First World War. Today, it is still committed to understanding people's needs though, of course, times and people have changed. Now, as well as working with adults and adolescents, the Tavistock Clinic has a large department for children and families. This offers help to parents who are finding the challenging task of bringing up their children daunting and has, therefore, a wide experience of children of all ages. It is firmly committed to early intervention in the inevitable problems that arise as children grow up, and to the view that if difficulties are caught early enough, parents are the best people to help their children with them. Professional Staff of the Clinic were, therefore, pleased to be able to contribute to this series of books to describe the ordinary development of children, to help in spotting the growing pains and to provide ways that parents might think about their children's growth.

**Elsie Osborne** was senior psychology tutor in the Child and Family Department of the Tavistock Clinic where she was responsible for new developments in clinical and school-based work and in training. She also chaired the Department for some years, as well as taking part in many activities at a national level. Publications include (with Emilia Dowling) "The Family and the School" and (with Isca Wittenberg and Gianna Henry) "The Emotional Experience of Learning and Teaching".

# CONTENTS

# INTRODUCTION

Your seven year old is likely to have a sense of mastery which is well founded. The achievements since birth are consider-able: in speech and language; in self-control, including mus-cular development as well as control of feelings and behaviour; increased social skills in mixing with a wider range of people; and a greater understanding of the world around. Even with all the assistance that you, as parents, have given, they are quite remarkable.

Established at school, about to embark on a more formal approach to learning, making friends and managing a great deal for themselves, such as meal times, washing, dressing and many other aspects of everyday life, seven year olds can seem well on the way to independence.

This book will try to share your pleasure in these achievements and to offer some further understanding of the tasks now facing the school child at this age, and what tensions and worries they might raise.

Two aspects around settling at school seem especially important. First of all the nature of the relationship between home and school. Home remains the important anchor, the secure base from which your seven year old can go out and explore the world. There is a bonus for parents and teachers if their relationship is reasonably harmonious but, as always in these books, the focus will be on the children themselves, the boys and girls who are having to manage to hold a balance between the two most important areas of their lives, home and school.

Another aspect of considerable importance is a tendency for differences between children to become more marked, and for comparisons between them increasingly to be made, particularly over progress in school work, including reading and writing skills, of course. So important indeed is the ability to read that we take a very special look at that.

There is also an expectation that children will be able to get on with each other more easily, and so comparisons to do with making friends and popularity are common as well.

These comparisons tend to be made with an idea of what is normal, against which every child is to be measured. Yet this preoccupation with what is average and desirable comes just when individual differences between children are becoming increasingly established. The sheer range of achievements that are becoming possible, the number of fresh interests that are being introduced mean that development cannot be identical for all children between their seventh and eighth birthdays. In any case, as parents already know, their children's characters and personalities are unique, and contrast increasingly evident, even within the same family.

In discussing, therefore, the areas of development

common to seven year olds, we will try to remember that, nevertheless, all children are different, not only in their range of intellectual abilities, their interests and social skills, but also in their emotional lives and capacity to cope with problems.

The aim of this series of books is to extend your understanding of your own child. We hope to do this by looking at seven year olds at home as well as at school, at play as well as at work, and the development of their own understanding of the world around them.

# CHAPTER ONE

# YOUR COMPETENT 7 YEAR OLD

## Becoming independent

Laura wants to go to school by herself. Her mother recognises that in the last year she has grown into a very sensible girl. All the same she thinks she is still too young to make the journey alone. Although she trusts Laura her mother thinks that there are still dangers she might not appreciate.

Such questions are typical of this year. Each parent will work out their own answer, taking into account their assessment of their own child and of local circumstances. Is the school just down the road? Are there major roads to be crossed? Is there a lonely footpath? Are there older brothers or sisters for company?

Parents are still making the important decisions but the fact that a question like this can arise is an illustration of how much the seven year old has grown in independence. Central to many parental concerns, therefore, is how to get the right balance between offering enough care and control while at the same time encouraging independence.

What are the developments and achievements on which this sense of the newly competent school boy or girl are based? Growth in height and strength of course. Greater manual skill and general control of their bodies, and many other physical developments. However what we really have in mind when we describe a child as sensible is related to the huge strides in understanding and awareness that have been made in the previous seven years.

It is with these mental aspects of growth, together with their emotional and social implications, that this chapter will be mainly concerned. Understanding these may also help a parent in making some of the big decisions referred to above.

## Understanding yourself and others

The description of Laura as "sensible" is a useful shorthand for much of this mental growth. In the past year Laura has achieved a much greater sense of herself as a distinct and separate person.

What is the nature of that important achievement? Throughout her childhood Laura has had a growing curiosity about herself and how her own mind works. She has acquired a greater awareness of her own experiences, she understands better the kind of feelings various experiences raise in her. She is also more confident in her understanding of reality.

Along with this clearer idea of her own identity, Laura has a level of self esteem which also gives her confidence. That self esteem has grown through the experience of opportunities to explore successfully, encouraged and supported by her parents throughout her early childhood.

This positive idea of who she is goes along with a better understanding of other people too. Understanding that other people have separate thoughts, wishes, feelings and intentions is a very special and important development in children's thinking. Somewhere around the age of seven this seems to become fairly well established.

Both at home and at school this increased ability of children to understand the needs of other people is largely taken for granted. The adults concerned probably do not worry all that much about what makes it possible. However such an immense shift in development is not going to be achieved completely in one stride.

Laura will not immediately understand why her parents take a different view to her on the question of going to school on her own. She argues with her mother: other children are allowed to go by themselves; she knows the way; the other children will think she is a baby, and so on. Faced with all these arguments her mother is tempted to say "no, you can't go to school on your own yet, because I say so".

It is easy to sympathise with a parent exasperated by an argumentative seven year old. Still, it is worth remembering that learning to argue by using reason is in fact a big improvement on the old temper tantrums and stubborn insistence of earlier years!

In the end her mother made an agreement to take Laura within a safe distance from where she could go on to school alone.

Of course Laura's arguments suggest her growing sense of, and wish for, more independence. They also suggest some of the new pressures she is now experiencing. Clearly many of these come from the greater demands of school, but also, in a different way, from home. In addition there are all the issues arising from measuring herself against her classmates and friends, the peers with whom she now spends so much of her day.

In making a compromise over the journey to school her mother shows a willingness to recognise both Laura's need for independence and her need for a continuing sense of security.

# The importance of language

So much of the development described in this chapter goes along with an increasing use of language that it seems important to give it special attention. Most seven year olds will now have a vocabulary of several thousand words. Of course they can only use the words they have heard, and now very often those they have read, but how they use them is not just through imitation. Just how children learn to use language, to invent their own sentences is still a matter of debate but the effect is enormous. A whole new world of learning opens up.

When he started school a couple of years ago Tom could already manage many things for himself and make use of quite a wide vocabulary. Now, like most seven year olds, his knowledge of words is increasing daily. Discovering new words is a delight. Having heard the word "competent" for the first time one day at home, he could be heard saying it to himself over and over with his own distinctive pronunciation, "combitent".

The words Tom understands best are, however, still those that relate to something that can be described, or imagined, in some way that is close to his own experience. When told to cut his food up properly he knows very well what the word "cut" means, but he was puzzled when he heard his parents saying of somebody they knew, "poor Harry, everybody cut him dead", when Harry was still clearly alive.

Tom is only slowly coming to understand such metaphors, as well as more abstract ideas. He knows that cats, dogs and rabbits, with which he is very familiar, are all animals, but he also knows that there are many, many more animals, some of which he has never seen, even in a picture book or on TV.

Sooty is his family's cat, and an important part of Tom's everyday experience. Sorting out just how the cat is also an animal, like other animals which are *not* cats, is not part of first hand experience in the same way. Tom has learned by thinking about it.

Perhaps one way of understanding the progress that has been made is to compare Tom now with how he was at four. He was trying to sort out some mixed up sets of cards which had animals and fruits on them. He knew all of them by name but he finished up with a very haphazard result. His father tried to get him to explain the way he had sorted them out but Tom could not.

Nowadays he does similar sorting problems without any difficulty and can give a good reason for what he has done.

Most of his friends are also good at doing this kind of thing now, although they might find different ways of doing it, and sometimes their ideas might not be what we expected. For instance, one boy divided all the fruits and all the animals into their separate piles but then explained that the animal pile was put together because they were things that chased each other, like cats chase mice. Whatever the explanation there will usually be some reasoning at work which we as adults can understand.

Tom also understands a great deal about time. He can tell you about his holiday visit to the seaside, and look forward to the fact that he has a swimming class on Thursday, but tell him that he only has five more minutes in which to clear up and his sense of time does not seem nearly so good.

Tom can be quite skilful at delaying tactics when it suits him, but it is also true that estimating the duration of time really is much more difficult than understanding that time exists, that there is yesterday, today and tomorrow. How often do we all underestimate or overestimate the amount of time that has passed, according to whether we are bored, anxious or really involved in something? Tom's mother has learned certain tactics of her own, of course, such as "I want you to have started clearing up by the time I have counted ten!"

These developments are all aided now by your child's knowledge of the correct words to express them. Without those words many ideas could not be exchanged or explained.

The wonderful and fascinating development of language is a subject that could, and has, filled many books. It is bound to come up again but for the moment we should move on to look at other aspects of your seven year old's remarkable competence.

## Sorting out the "real world"

Both Laura and Tom have an increasing understanding of the world, of what is real and what is pretend. When she was four Laura said that the cherry stalks had jumped off her plate onto the floor; now when she is reminded of it, she says that it was silly.

She no longer accepts that all sorts of objects can be treated as if they are alive in the same way. As adults we might talk of the weather as though it was deliberately spoiling some activity we had planned, or speak of a smile on the moon's face, but this is usually done with a sense of humour or maybe, in the second case, as a poetic kind of notion. It is with this sense of fun that Tom and Laura share a new approach to make believe.

At their age they are less easily fooled by pretence and disguise. They may still enjoy Father Christmas, but this will be more likely because they choose to join in the make believe.

Of course, it is also quite useful still to believe in the tooth fairy, who leaves a coin under your pillow in place of a lost tooth.

Like almost all children of their age they enjoy animal stories, but now they do not treat animals as people in the same way as they used to. They may still enjoy stories in which animals talk and have feelings, but they know they are pretending. Sometimes this use of animals can be seen as a way of creating a more manageable world. Some of the most popular children's books, especially the so-called classics, like Alice in Wonderland, Black Beauty, The Wind in the Willows, The Just So stories, and many, many more have made use of this enjoyment of animal make believe.

The capacity to pretend in a new way will come up again when looking at the seven year old at play. Play at this age also involves coming to terms with other people in a more mature way.

## Social skills

What competence have Tom and Laura developed in their social relationships? Now, at seven, they have a better understanding of themselves and of other people's thoughts and feelings, and they feel more secure in the "real world". As a result it is easier for them to take turns and to wait for their share of attention.

In the classroom the teacher is much more able to treat the children as a group. Of course, children vary in how sociable they are, and most still like some time to themselves. The greater social sense which is being described here is something different. Indeed, seven year olds are not generally attracted in a big way by larger group activities, that will become much more important in another year or two.

The kind of social understanding we have in mind is a greater ability to make allowances for other people, to understand that there are rules in a group and to accept the reasonable discipline this involves.

There is still a great deal of pleasure in free and spontaneous behaviour in play and other ways, in creating and exploring new things. That spontaneity, which is one of the delights of childhood, still needs space for expression.

Greater social understanding also does not rule out competition and rivalry between classmates and between brothers and sisters. There will certainly be plenty of that. Indeed, quarrels seem to be a normal way of growing up. The author, G.K. Chesterton once said that people quarrel because they have not yet learned to argue. Well, Laura and Tom are already much more able to supply reasons to support their point of view, as we have already seen in Laura's case. Now maybe they can increasingly grow away from quarrelling towards argument. Not all adults have quite got to that point either as yet!

If competition is evident, so also is co-operation. When the small group at Laura's and Tom's table was given the task by the teacher of making a poster, they all needed some help to share the work out at first, but then they were often seen to be busy giving help and advice to each other. For example, on where to place parts of the picture and how to spell words.

Friendships are likely to come and go and membership of groups to shift around. As already noted comparisons with other children are frequently made, what they do and what their parents allow.

This leads us to the difficult question of standards and expectations, of what is average or normal. We will return to this topic in the chapter on school.

## Plain sailing?

If the emphasis upon the achievements of seven year olds suggests that all the big problems of growing up are, at least for the moment, overcome, then any parent will hasten to disagree. Seven does seem to be a sort of landmark in the change from infancy to schoolchild and so the problems of seven year olds change accordingly.

Parents may find many of these new accomplishments a mixed blessing. Seven year olds can be a worry as they demand more independence, and they can be wearing with their greater skills in arguing, demanding reasons and con-stantly drawing on their wider range of experiences to make comparisons.

The children themselves find that there are new de-mands on them, less tolerance of their individual fads, more insistence on keeping to the rules, and it can be a struggle to keep up their own self esteem in the light of all these, especially when there are also many new comparisons being made with other children.

Confidence therefore may well swing between too much certainty, based on new found skills, and too little when performance does not come up to expectations. This is a time when children can be very self critical and also sensitive to other people's comments. The developments which have been described have still many ups and downs in being applied to everyday life.

Seven year olds are still learning about the give and take of relationships in the light of their increased understanding of other people, and some allowances are likely to be needed. They know that others have feelings, as they do, but they cannot yet put themselves into somebody else's shoes in a fully grown up way.

The capacity to understand is there, but that is not the same as acquiring settled habits. Reminders to "wait until you are asked" are likely to be as necessary as reminders "to wipe your feet".

The problems will be different at home and at school and, as these two worlds become more separate, there will be the need to find ways of managing the link between them. There are times when children can be put in the position of "piggy-in-the-middle". Even when relationships between home and school are at their smoothest your seven year old has to be a kind of go-between, shifting from one set of rules and customs to another.

When Tom fell and cut his knee at school his teacher said that he behaved very bravely. The tears did not come until he was safely at home and his mother took the bandage off to have a look. When Laura was angry because her pencils were broken by another girl at school, her real feelings were expressed when she shouted at her mother that she needed new ones *now*. Home is the place where we can safely "let go" and know that we will be forgiven. Seven year olds are no different from most of us in reserving much of our worst behaviour for those we love best.

# CHAPTER TWO

# YOUR 7 YEAR OLD AT HOME

## Relationships in the family

Keith and Robin are brothers. Keith is nine and a half years old and Robin is just seven. Keith is rather quiet and something of a worrier. For instance, he worries if he has not got exactly the right shoes for games, he becomes anxious over holiday plans and wants to know what to expect in advance. Robin is exuberant and adventurous, his words tumble over themselves at times and his main worry is about when he can get outside to play.

Father took both boys to the park one Saturday afternoon with their bicycles. Robin rode his as fast as he could, getting up speed in order to copy the older children, who were going up on the back wheels of their bikes. Suddenly, as he tried to do the same thing, he fell off, giving his head quite a bang. He wanted to see mummy.

Father put the two boys into the car and took them straight home. It was Keith, rather pale, who was most anxious to explain to mummy what had happened and how Robin had been showing off. Once it was clear that no serious harm had been done and Robin had been comforted, his mother asked him what he had been trying to do, and why. Robin explained what he had been watching the other boys doing and how he had tried to do the same because "it looked such good fun". Almost immediately he was keen to get back on his bike again.

Their parents wonder how they can have two boys who are so opposite in character. Like so many parents before them, they try to make the most of the positive sides of both children, but they also have separate worries about each of them.

Mother said that in many ways Robin had been good for Keith, who had been encouraged, perhaps even goaded, by Robin into being a bit more adventurous. On the other hand, Keith could be relied upon to tell Robin off when he wanted to do something which Keith thought was stupid.

However, Keith is not always just a quiet, rather shy, amenable boy. He can be stubborn and awkward. Mostly this comes from his wish to have everything orderly. At his seventh birthday party he had become very upset when the game was not being played according to his rules. His mother has discovered since he started school that he is not at his best in large groups of children. She has also found that parties for him need to have plenty of clearly organised activities.

Robin certainly needs supervision still, and sometimes has to be restrained. His daring behaviour is a worry at times, but his mother rather enjoys his adventurous spirit and does not want to quell it. She did hope that the fall off the bicycle might have taught him a bit of a lesson, but such bumps do not seem to make all that much difference to Robin.

Fortunately even adventurous boys like Robin, by the

age of seven have a reasonable understanding of how far they can go and will try to remain safe enough. Firm and clear boundaries set by their parents can be accepted surprisingly well.

This is where the huge increase in the use and understanding of language is an advantage for parents too. Demands can be justified and the results of misdeeds put into words. So far as Robin is concerned his mother puts them in a much more dramatic form than she would to Keith, in order to reinforce her rules.

It is more likely to be father who gets impatient with Robin. A quiet, thoughtful man himself, he has usually got on well with his older son, and is good at getting through to Keith when he is in one of his difficult moods.

Both boys can still show affection and warmth to their mother. When Keith was seven he would sit close to his mother and tell her she looked pretty. Now, at the same age, Robin will come home from school and give his mother a hug in his usual exuberant way. Robin's mixture of toughness and sweetness makes him very endearing to her.

With such different behaviour within the same family, how much greater the variations must be across families in general. What generalisations could possibly apply to everybody? Probably none!

# Getting on with parents

All the same there are some features of family relationships that seem general enough at this age. For instance, even though there is a lot of variation amongst children in how much they directly involve their parents in their activities, there is, by seven, an increasing tendency for their play to be with other children and to exclude their parents.

At four Tom used to involve his mother in playing with him. He liked her to take a part in his games of imagination. Looking back, she recalls rather ruefully how she used to have to be the gangster being captured by policeman hero Tom, but now she just occasionally gets asked to play a card game when there are no friends around.

This is part of a wider change in the relationship between children and their parents at this age, with more distinction being made between boys and girls. Laura's mother enjoys a new kind of companionship with her daughter. They go shopping together and have long chats which makes Laura feel pretty grown up.

Keith and Robin's father, as we saw, takes his sons on outings by himself, and especially enjoys their regular visits to the local swimming pool, and sees the great pleasure the boys themselves have in having his attention to themselves.

This pleasure in watching their children growing up adds to the respect these parents have for them as individuals. Keith and Robin have grown up with a reasonable experience of being listened to, being given some choice whenever possible, and of being allowed some space which was absolutely their own to keep their belongings. These experiences have been important in providing a basis for a new kind of friendly relationship between parents and children, now that the old, dependent one of infancy is fading.

In Keith and Robin's family it was an advantage to have parents who complemented each other, one coping more easily with Keith, the other with Robin. In other ways too it can be useful to have two parents who counterbalance each other.

It is hard, if not impossible, for children to grow up

happily in a home where mother and father have frequent, angry quarrels. Constant, unspoken hostility between them, or a relationship in which one domineers over the other are no better. Children are likely to take sides, openly or secretly, with feelings of hate, scorn and anger which can be powerful and enduring.

Where parents disagree about them, children may discover how to play one off against the other. As a result parents can make great efforts always to appear in perfect agreement, especially supporting each other over matters of discipline. If, however, the parental partners can accept that there are bound to be occasions when they disagree, and yet in spite of this can show that they continue to respect each other, their children are unlikely to suffer too much, may find they have a useful example to follow, and benefit from an idea of authority which is not too absolute.

Seven year olds ask different kinds of questions of their parents. The earlier questioning about babies, how they are made, where they come from, the differences between boys and girls have generally subsided. Hopefully, they have been answered well enough. This is not to say that all interest in these matters has gone, to reappear only in adolescence.

Your seven year old observes the adult world more acutely than might sometimes appear to be the case. There will be uncertainties which still need to be explored and questions asked. Sexual identity is part of the general picture of themselves that boys and girls have, and interest in it is natural and continuing.

There is another side to the rather harmonious picture that has been presented here. Parents remain the principal target for stormier feelings. The increase in tact, in awareness of others and in control of feelings which takes place during this year is much more evident in public than in private behaviour. On the whole, however, most parents probably prefer it that way round.

There is no one kind of home that guarantees happiness of course. Equally happy homes can have different atmospheres which are dependant on many things. Some of these will be to do with material aspects, how well-off the family is, how big the house they live in, how much private space is possible, whether there is a garden. Others will be to do with the structure of the family, the number of children, whether both parents are working and what visitors come from elsewhere.

There will also be the preferences which influence the family's habits and customs. Some will be highly organised and orderly, others easy going, in some the emphasis will be on individual responsibility, in others a strong feeling for acting as a united family, and so far as discipline is concerned there is a wide range from the very strict to the very permissive.

In Leslie's case there was a minimum of control. His family was artistic and easy-going, and the children were well-loved. Yet he started to have nightmares in which he was in frightening situations where he could do nothing. On the other hand at school he was creative and getting on well. Two stories which he told about some pictures illustrate his dilemma.

In the first he described how some chicks organised their own picnic, and when they had finished made their own decision as to whether to get any more food. When mother hen came and told them it was time to go home they cleared up and carried everything back.

This story seems to describe very well how self-reliant

Leslie was, with mother safely in the background. The next story showed that underneath he could still get frightened and need his mother to be more readily available.

This second story was about a baby rabbit who one night asked the mummy rabbit if he could go to bed, and she said "of course, you don't need to ask me". But when he was in bed the rabbit called out "I saw a ghost, I'm scared". So his mummy came and turned on the light, and he saw it was only a chair with a white cloth over it. And so he went to sleep.

Leslie's independence was not yet all that secure and it seemed he was worried about being left to make too many decisions for himself. Still, mother did come to the little frightened rabbit in his story and, in Leslie's own very affectionate family, the long term prospect seemed a happy one.

A major focus of the relationship between parents and children now arises from the shared interest in school. Parents can find themselves apparently being compared with the teacher and found wanting, in knowledge, in authority and in judgment. The strong attachment made to the teacher is a reflection of her (or, less often, him) taking over some parental responsibility. It is also true that if Laura and Tom like their teacher they are more likely to be able to learn successfully from her.

All the same, however likeable and friendly the teacher is, her role is a formal one which, in the end, makes it quite unlike the relationship to mummy and daddy at home. Teachers do not as a rule enter their profession because of an urge to become substitute parents. Many of them may be parents themselves, and only too well aware of the different roles they have in their two jobs at home and in the classroom.

The opportunity for a new, intense, yet less emotion-

who will in turn have the pleasure of being the big grown up, with a great boost to self-esteem. That is, just as long as the responsibility does not go too far, or carry on for too long!

When a new baby is expected, the seven year old is well able to share in the family's anticipation and in the baby's arrival. Jealousy of the new baby is generally not too serious a problem and it is possible to involve the seven year old in a helpful way. There can be exceptions, of course.

Bobby became attention-seeking at school, complaining that he could not work because other children were interfering with him. He lived with his parents and two other children in a small flat. When a new baby arrived his mother was harassed, trying to keep their crowded home clean and tidy whilst hoping for new housing. Bobby's mother varied between expecting him, as the eldest, to be helpful and grown up, and treating him as too young to be really trusted. Talking things over with friends gave this mother a chance to see what was happening before it got out of hand.

Once at school, most friends are likely to be chosen from classmates or other children of similar age. This will be reinforced as your child is increasingly able to move around more independently and exercise more independent choice. Brothers and sisters, however, remain immensely important for most children, for mutual support and the freedom to be themselves in a special way.

The sharing of joys and sorrows and the intensity of those shared experiences can, and often do, create a warmth and a bond between siblings which last long after childhood is past.

# Grandparents

It is worth thinking a little about the special contribution that grandparents make to children's development. The practical help that they often give to a family is clear enough, when they act as substitute parents and as babysitters, taking over in an emergency or providing a nearby second home.

Even when they live too far away for that to be possible, they can still be important figures for their grandchildren. Visited during holidays, they may also provide the first place where children stay away without their parents. For a girl from a big family the experience of staying on her own with her grandparents from time to time, was a treasured memory.

On top of that they bring a special quality to their grandchildren's experience of adults, especially of a sort of benign authority which is often remembered affectionately in later life. This is not necessarily because children are more indulged by grandparents, although to some extent they may be; there are often also quite definite rules. Kind but firm seems to be fine from grandparents, whereas parents in the same sort of situation get bickering and wheedling.

Both sides, grandparents and grandchildren can find reassurance and pleasure in the sense of continuity that goes with this important relationship, not only ongoing in the present, but linking back to the past. This sense of history may not be clearly specified but is there just the same.

Grandparents confirm that they often can manage their grandchildren better than they could their own children. Laura's grandma said that she had no idea how much she would really enjoy being a grandmother. The same thing must be true for many grandfathers who often have more chance to spend time with their children's children than they ever had with their own sons and daughters.

## Divorce and Step–Families

Much has been written about the effects of divorce on children, and it has been referred to in earlier books in this series. The separation of their parents continues to be an immensely disturbing event for a seven year old. In one sense, because of the child's better language, it will be easier to explain what is happening, although, in practice, parents may not find the right words all that readily.

An explanation of the reason for their separation may be just confusing. What their child probably needs is an account, which is as straightforward as possible, of what changes it will mean and a reassurance of the continuing love of both their parents.

Access arrangements can be better understood at seven than with a younger child, and this also means that a failure to keep to them will certainly be noted. In understanding your seven year old it might help to remember how difficult it is for a child at this age to cope with mixed feelings, especially when they are contradictory. So holding on to the idea of still loving somebody when you are angry with them is not really manageable. In addition the seven year old needs to be protected from the bitter feelings which may be around.

In Sharon's case she tried to protect herself from knowing what was going on. She shut herself away from the rows between her parents, apparently did not see or hear what was happening and denied to everybody that mummy and daddy were separating. The effect of this on her ability to learn was, however, devastating. Not only was Sharon too preoccupied with her worries to attend properly to school but it actually seemed that finding out about anything had become dangerous. Although she could already read quite a bit she now refused to do so.

Not until the arrangements for her future had been made clear and certain to her, could Sharon begin to pick up her life again. Slowly, with the help of a sympathetic teacher, she returned to learning.

Where there has been a divorce earlier then the chances are high that by the age of seven there will be a new family, a step-parent, maybe two if both parents have found new partners, but also step-sisters and brothers as well perhaps.

Added to the adjustment that this will mean for the children of both families, could be the arrival, at some later date, of a baby to the new partners.

If this begins to sound complicated to us we may imagine the problems it presents to a seven year old. Amongst the gaps in understanding and knowledge are some which we might find rather surprising. Outside the relationships of the immediate family, that is to say mother and father, brothers and sisters, the child of seven is still rather hazy.

Laura, our accomplished seven year old, knows her grandma very well, she lives nearby and Laura often spends a day with her on her own, especially during the holidays. She has learned that grandma is mummy's mother. Laura also has a favourite aunt Jane who is her mother's sister, but she was totally defeated by the question, "who is auntie Jane's mummy?"

How difficult it must often be to work out the relationships in a step-family. Children need help to work them out and are likely to be baffled by just being told, "now you have a new family". This idea that the family, the main source of certainty and security, can change so radically is unsettling, at the very least.

Of course it is a difficult time for the adults too, but it is worth the effort to look at things from a child's perspective for a while. If the children can accept and live with the new arrangements then life will certainly be easier for the new parental couple.

In Angela's case it was by chance that her teacher discovered that part of her distress about her new step-father was because of her belief that she could not love two fathers at once. The teacher shared this discovery with Angela's mother. Reassured that it was perfectly all right to go on loving her old daddy, and reminded that he still loved her, Angela was helped to feel less muddled, which allowed her to work better again at school, the problem that had first worried her teacher.

This did not solve everything for Angela though. She continued to nurse the hope, as many other children do, that her original parents would come together again. This was not entirely given up but her step-father worked hard at getting on with her and she was able to enjoy her visits to her natural father.

It is not only the children who can cherish hopes of re-establishing some lost ideal. Parents may also dream of a new perfect family and expect that the children will welcome having a new father or mother, to share their activities and to look after them. The failure to appreciate some of the problems that are inevitable in setting up a new family means that the effect of the changes for the children cannot be anticipated, and they then cannot be prepared for their new life in a realistic way.

Not all children are as lucky as Angela, who received

understanding from the adults involved once they realised how confused she was. She was allowed to choose which surname to use and preferred to keep her father's name for a long time. She was living in a new house but was still able to go to the same school. The changes were still considerable, but they were manageable.

These suggest just a few of the additional problems that some children might face. Seven year old Michael went to live in his step-father's house, with his five year old sister Maureen. His mother had been divorced for the past two years and he had learned to be the helpful son when his mother found part-time work.

The new family included his step-father's son, Andrew, now ten years old. Andrew's mother had been killed in a street accident four years earlier and father and son had grieved for her together. Now he hoped that they would find happiness with his new wife. He had explained to Andrew how he loved her and hoped Andrew would love her as well.

Instead there was considerable bickering, which finally threatened to destroy the marriage, and help was sought in family therapy. The feelings which emerged included a great deal of anger. Michael was displaced from his position as the eldest child and deeply resented Andrew. Andrew reminded him that he was younger and treated him in many ways as an intruder. Andrew hated having to share his room with Michael, and compared Michael's mother unfavourably with his own. He also felt that Maureen was being spoiled by his father. In addition Maureen did not want to share her mother with Andrew, a feeling which was intensified by the fact that she was having to move from the nursery school which she had known for the last two years.

Of course step-families have the same sort of problems

as original families, and the personalities within them are as varied, but they do have some aspects which are special to them also.

Exploring in advance what sort of changes there could be, and then sharing these with the children, might at least make it more possible to cope with them. It may also help to remember that many of these will seem small, but potentially be causes of the greatest irritation of all. Two life-styles have to be brought together and two sets of family customs somehow combined.

The growth in the number of step-families have made them an important topic, which we are still learning to understand better. There is no point in blaming fairy stories for the bad reputation they give to step-families, although we can note that many of the most popular ones include wicked step-mothers, Cinderella, Snow White, Hansel and Gretel for example. Such stories go back many centuries and still have strong appeal. Maybe we can understand them as an illustration of the universal need to have a clear division between good and bad, between heroes and villains, a dilemma which has always preoccupied people. If the wicked step-mother became the one who could be loaded with all the bad parts this could allow the real, but absent, mother to remain absolutely good.

As noted already, seven year olds do not find it easy to recognise mixed feelings, but we can help them to accept that in the real world nobody is all good or all bad. The fairy stories will continue to have their place in reassuring children that good can win.

# Independence and control

Alongside the question of how much independence to allow your seven year old is the equally difficult one of how much control to exercise. Some comments on this have already been offered. For instance, the greater ability of the seven year old to understand language means that it is much easier to accept discipline through reasoning. A parent can offer explanations as well as instructions, can justify their demands as well as expect a certain level of routine obedience. At this age a child can more easily anticipate the consequences of an action, and a parent can reinforce this awareness with warnings of bad outcomes and predictions of good ones.

Now is a time when this more enlightened discipline really begins to pay off. Alas, bad habits of control are not easily broken. Sam, for instance had been habitually smacked. His busy mother had found through the years that she could get results when she eventually reinforced her demands with a slap. Now, at seven, Sam did not really listen until the slap came. For him it was a matter of waiting for smacking as the signal to comply. Yet Sam's mother herself admitted that she never really used smacking as a punishment, but rather as the quickest way of "getting through to him", when she was short of time and temper.

This habitual use of smacking to gain compliance also meant that it lost any force to shock Sam when he had behaved in a really naughty way, spitefully teasing his younger sister.

Independence is only possible as self-control develops. It is not just a matter of being allowed to do more things on your own. Independence equally means taking responsibility for yourself. In practical, everyday terms it is reflected in such things as knowing how to behave when out to tea, how to answer the 'phone, what to do when travelling on the bus and when going on an outing.

Seven year olds are still fearful of getting lost but in fact are much less likely to become lost than younger children, partly because they now look ahead more readily, and partly because they can understand other people's actions and see the need for rules and boundaries more easily. If, in spite of all that, they do get lost, they are now better able to deal with it sensibly, by going to an adult in authority for instance.

Amongst the hazards most parents try to prepare their children to deal with are crossing roads and watching out for traffic. The rules for these are usually quite definite and until they are understood, and seen to be obeyed, going out without a familiar adult or responsible older sibling is unlikely to be allowed.

.Another worry about your child going out alone is that of behaving sensibly when strangers approach them, and the rules about this are more difficult to convey, because they require a more advanced sort of understanding. Teaching a practical caution, without making a child fearful of every unfamiliar person is a challenge. A balance has to be made between setting out some rules in a business-like way and not being too frightening.

These instructions cannot be quite so readily set out as they can for crossing the road. How you tell your child about the dangers of accepting lifts or offers of sweets from strangers will depend so much on your judgment of your own child. Do you just repeat the rule, "never speak to strangers", or do you discuss with them their right to say "no", or do they need to be made just a bit more alarmed than that? How do you make sure that you do not transfer all your worst fears to them?

Rules about coming straight home from school are

amongst the most common and the strictest in being applied. How many mothers have found their submerged fears coming to the surface when their child is late home? Some of the parents we have been describing saved their hardest punishments for occasions when a child went off to play with a friend without telling them first, or stopped to go into the local shop and dallied over the comics. Most parents could supply examples of the excuses that are provided.

Over the next few years, as your child grows up, issues of this kind will be more and more prominent. In the end the way they are managed will depend on your assessment of your own child. There is no certain, universal rule, but it does make sense to start creating habits of thought and action during this year. In later years there might be a more explosive demand for independence.

## Pocket money

A different aspect of independence is signified by pocket money. Any parent who can afford it is likely to offer some pocket money, usually as of right, but maybe earned, or added to by being rewarded for useful jobs around the house.

Most parents are also keen to see this as an opportunity to learn to use money sensibly. Keith and Robin's mother found her own way of encouraging this. She said that she discovered jumble sales as a way of keeping her two boys, with their different interests, happily occupied for some time during many week-ends.

She also found that giving them 50 pence to spend however they liked not only kept them busy scurrying around but had other benefits too. The agreement was that she would not interfere at all with their choice. This meant that she sometimes had difficulty holding her tongue, but she offered neither advice nor criticism. Very quickly both boys had learned to hold on to their money until they had had a good look round. They had debates together about the best bargains, discovered that if they waited until near the end some things got cheaper, and faced hard decisions over spending all their money on one highly desired item.

Other parents too find creative ways of helping their children contain their first impulsive wishes to buy, followed by regrets, and pleas for just a bit more for something special. Making this task fun as well requires some parental imagination. Observing how her children responded gave the mother of these two boys a feeling of success and pleasure.

# CHAPTER THREE

# YOUR 7 YEAR OLD AT SCHOOL

## Relationship with the teacher

A certain amount of competition and rivalry between home and school and between parents and teachers has already been mentioned. This can be a source of conflict and tension, especially for the child who is caught in a battle between these two most important areas in his life. At the same time parents want the relationship between their child and the teacher to be good and positive. They recognise how important this is in their child's progress at school. And they are right.

In order to understand the nature of this relationship better it might be useful to recall your own early days at school. It is likely that amongst those recollections some of the most vivid will be around the teachers you had. Do you remember the teacher who made you feel secure, who kept the whole class busy and under control? The one who used sarcasm when you did something wrong, who kept order but nobody liked very much? Or the one where everybody played up and you didn't learn much; it seemed like a bit of fun, but it was a relief when another teacher took over?

Although many things may have changed at school since your days there, most of the feelings involved will have stayed the same. No doubt many children will become adults who look back and remember the teacher whose approval made all the difference to their life at school or to the subject they loved.

In a strange situation, amongst unfamiliar children, uncertain and therefore a bit lost, it must be immensely reassuring to find an adult who takes control and offers you interesting things to do. When this new adult then appears to be reliably there every day, knows who you are, calls you by name and seems to care what happens, we can see how the beginnings of a new attachment to an adult are made.

The special authority that the teacher has is emphasised by the fact that they are in charge of a whole class. The teacher is also helped by the increasing social understanding and ability to accept a more formal way of learning of the children themselves.

Throughout the junior school years the teachers continue to have a kind of caring and looking after role, but their main purpose is in their teaching and in the children's achievement. Their central aim is distinct from a mothering one, but much discomfort arises from confusion between these two roles.

In these first years at school attachments to teachers can be especially strong. Having to move on to a new teacher, leaving behind one that was very much liked, is reflected in a common worry for parents. For Shirley it felt quite devastating. Her mother was bringing up Shirley and her younger brother single-handed. She was working part-time and therefore greatly relieved when Shirley went off happily to school and was proud of her independent little daughter.

Shirley became very fond of one of her teachers in particular, a warm, motherly person, with whom she kept contact all the time she was in the infants' school. At seven, she moved from the infants to the junior school, with a new, rather stern headmistress, as well as a new class teacher who expected more conformity.

Shirley became withdrawn and unhappy, and stopped talking about school when she came home. One day, however, her mother overheard her talking to her teddy bear, harsh and angry with this much loved toy. Her mother sympathised with the poor teddy bear and picked it up gently. Suddenly all Shirley's feelings of unhappiness about school came flooding out. As anger turned to tears mother gave her daughter a hug, and it seemed from that moment that Shirley felt she was given permission to take her worries home again.

Her mother realised, with regret, just how much of a shock the transfer had been for Shirley. Although she had been aware that the new school was quite a big change she had been confident that Shirley liked school and would soon settle down again. The infants' school teacher had felt aware of Shirley's wish for mothering, but had allowed this to become a rather too dependant relationship, and had not been able to help her to let go.

There are other aspects of the earlier relationship to parents that can get transferred to teachers. Most small children have an idea of their parents as knowing everything, of being very powerful. This can only too readily be transferred to teachers, who are specifically supposed to pass on knowledge and learning. But the good teacher wants to do something else, which is to help the children to think for themselves, to be curious, to try to work things out and find answers, and to use their skills in creative ways.

This is not necessarily helped by the kind of teacher who always knows everything and cannot leave space for the children to find out. A good preparation will also have been made by parents who themselves have allowed a child room to think and explore, and been willing to accept their own limitations. Then their children have a model of someone they respect who does not have to be all-powerful, someone they can trust to answer their questions truthfully and reliably.

Teachers do make extraordinary attempts to be all things to all children. Keith's teacher allowed him to lean against her while they looked at his reading book together, and he found her comforting when he was upset. The same teacher, when she had Robin, was challenging in a rather jokey way. Other children have different personalities, shy children who need encouragement to build their confidence, quick children who want constant stimulation, slower children who need time. Teachers have their own personalities too and take more readily to some styles than others. In a way it is remarkable that most children do settle down with the teacher they have, and do get on with the job of learning.

## What does settling down mean?

Settling down at school is accepted as being in everybody's interest, teachers, parents and children. Some of the developments that make this possible have already been talked about throughout this book. They include intellectual, social and emotional growth, the influence of previous experiences and the expectations of society, as represented by their own families and most other people they come in contact with.

Settling down implies accepting the authority of school

and the restrictions that are inevitable in a large organisation. It means making allowances for other children, finding your way about, both in terms of the building itself, and in terms of the rules of the group and its values.

The demands all this adjustment makes on your particular seven year old are increasing at this age and throughout junior school. It is only possible for the great majority of children to meet them because there are also satisfactions and rewards which come as a result of coping successfully with these new demands.

Self-esteem is enhanced as new skills are learned and achievements registered. Not least among these are the new social skills. The satisfactions of being part of a group can be considerable, and learning to manage the difficulties that can also arise within a group will serve a child well in the future.

This sense of being part of a group, with its order and routines is one of the things that make it possible for one teacher alone to work with a whole classroom of children, without having to be a tyrant.

## Learning and the curriculum.

A lot of use has been made of the word "learning" in this book. it is time to give some thought to the most usual sense in which it is used. That is to say to the "reading, writing and arithmetic" that is to be covered. There is a National Curriculum which most parents with school children will have heard of. In Britain it is still in a new and developing stage, but the overall intention is to replace the old informal setting of standards, monitored by the school Inspectorate, with a much more formal setting out of key stages in the teaching of every subject.

For seven year olds there are specific requirements not

only in the old "three R's", covered by English and maths, but also in science, technology, history and geography, which are all graded into levels and tested by Standard Assessment Tasks, as they are called. Art, music and physical education are also covered by specific activities and expectations at all ages, but are not tested in the same way.

There is still a lot of discussion, especially about the way in which seven year olds are tested, and no doubt changes will be made over time. The National Curriculum has not yet "settled down", and therefore has the possibility of being a disturbance as well as offering the advantages of setting general standards.

School reports for parents will have to cover all their child's levels in all the subjects, as well as those of the class in general, and such reports are likely to be quite complicated.

For most parents of seven year olds the easiest, and most important, yardstick of learning will remain their child's progress in reading. If that is not going well they know that all other subjects will be held up. The need to be able to read is so great that failure here is the greatest worry about school work that most parents have.

William's mother was convinced that he was dyslexic and she became involved in a battle about this at school. She insisted that William needed special help. The teacher argued that William did not have the usual indications of dyslexia and that there were other children in the class who were much more in need of extra help than her son. Caught between the two William quietly kept his head down.

The head teacher became aware of the situation and intervened to suggest that an independent assessment should be made by the educational psychologist who worked with the school. This was done and amongst her findings were some which threw light on the origins of the debate. Mother's anxiety could be better understood when it was realised that William's father had had considerable difficulty with learning to read as a child, and felt strongly that this had been neglected until it was almost too late. Although he could now read quite well he still got help from his wife with spelling. His wife was certain that he had been an unrecognised dyslexic.

The teacher, who was still quite new to his job, felt angry with a mother who claimed to know more about reading difficulties than he, the expert, did. Neither parent nor teacher was able to take a cool look at the real situation. William himself meanwhile was learning to evade work, rather than learning to read.

Reading is one of the first great tests of learning ability. Important though intelligence may be, learning involves a great deal more. To understand more of how learning takes place it is worth looking at the feelings involved. These include accepting that there are things that you do not already know, putting up with feelings of uncertainty, bearing frustration and disappointment when the learning is difficult and, finally, keeping alive the wish to learn in spite of failure.

The experience of failure may lead to other feelings, depending on the personality and the previous experiences of an individual child. Some children may respond with anxiety and evasion, as William did, others may give up through despair. Children who set off with high hopes may now feel that they are stupid, all of them are likely to be undermined by constant or harsh criticism or derision.

The National Curriculum is not only concerned with children acquiring facts and figures, good spelling and neat handwriting, there is a recognition also that learning requires habits of listening, observing, finding out and interpreting.

Teachers use many methods to make their lessons interesting, so that the facts will be understood and all these good habits acquired, but they also have to help their pupils remain motivated and survive failure, and that means managing some strong feelings at times.

If this is successfully done during this first year of formal schooling then a good start to all future learning has been made. No wonder the relationship to the teacher is regarded as important by the parents. Learning will never be an absolutely straight line of success, but it's route can and should be a rewarding one.

# What is normal?

School is above all the place where children are compared and compare themselves with others. The greater emphasis on testing and measuring children's achievement can seem to imply that there is a standard, a norm, that every child must reach. Knowing where your child's strengths and weaknesses lie can be very useful, but the pressure to be up to standard in every respect can become tyrannical. Too much preoccupation with norms can also mean that the special gifts of a particular child may be overlooked or ignored.

What is normal is usually taken to be what is average. Yet average is only a way of describing the middle of a whole range. It is unavoidable that some children will be above it and some will be below. This is easier to accept for some things, like height and weight, unless a child is at one extreme or the other. A teacher of many years experience once confided that he had a special sympathy for such children. By the time he was twelve, and had just moved up from junior school, he was six feet tall and he still remembered what a hard time he had as a result of this. The advantages were well outnumbered by the disadvantages since he was constantly expected to live up to his height rather than his age.

Now, as just an extra-tall adult, he recalled how much he had often wished to be shorter, and how long it took him to come to terms with always being the tallest in the class.

This teacher's example is a reminder of how much a child is affected by the expectations of others, and what uncomfortable pressures these can become when they are not appropriate. The teacher had been an intelligent schoolboy, but still he had felt pushed beyond what was reasonable.

He also provides us with a useful reminder that it is not always easy to be well above average. The mother of a seven year old who had been assessed as "gifted", that is of outstanding intelligence, was overwhelmed by the responsibility which she felt this description placed on her. She was a single mother by choice but at this time she said how much she missed a partner to discuss things with. She also felt it created something of a barrier to talking to other parents at school who might just feel she was being boastful. Talking to the teachers also made her feel awkward, seeming to ask for special arrangements in an inner city school that she knew was very hard-pressed.

The feeling that other parents, or the teachers, may be resentful of an outstandingly talented child probably does have some basis in experience. Amongst other ways, this can be expressed as an expectation that such children can get on all right by themselves. In many ways just being average and, therefore, part of the majority is more comfortable for the parents as well as the child.

The idea that every child can be measured against what is normal carries with it an additional idea that failure to meet that target means that something is wrong with the individual child. That can have an unpleasant labelling effect. The alternative to blaming a child for failure is to blame the teacher for using the wrong teaching method.

# Problems in learning to read

For instance there has always been discussion about the best method for teaching reading, with fashions coming and going for the one way which would be best for all children. In fact most teachers use a mixture of methods to teach and most children use a mixture of ways to learn, whether it is look and say, phonics, word building, word games, literacy and understanding, or anything else. An exclusive emphasis upon one method is almost certain to create difficulties for some children. Some approaches are more weighted towards providing attractive reading books, others to providing some rules for tackling new words.

The addition that this chapter has hoped to make is that feelings will also be an important part of successful learning. This is illustrated by Ben's story. Ben's mother had been ill in hospital and his father had looked after Ben at home. Ben became very difficult in class and his reading, from what had been a slow beginning was making no progress at all.

Ben's teacher was increasingly concerned and asked the parents to meet with him at school. Father came on his own and explained that mother had been very ill. He was surprised to hear that Ben was behaving badly at school since at home he had been very good and helpful. He had told Ben that Mummy had nearly died, and when she came home he would have to be very grown up, as they would both have to look after her.

This new picture coming from father suggested to the

teacher that maybe Ben was rather afraid of growing up and taking on this immense responsibility. It made sense of his reluctance to learn to read, or indeed do anything else, that would hasten this growing up. The teacher became interested in the pictures Ben sometimes drew, which did indeed suggest frightening catastrophes. He asked Ben to tell him the stories of the pictures and in these stories anxieties about the need for somebody to be in control became very clear.

The telling of the stories themselves, and the understanding they gave the teacher were in themselves helpful to Ben. The suggestion was also made to his father that less pressure be put on Ben at home, and more allowance made for his age. Less clear was the reason for his generally aggressive behaviour, but as the pressures eased this also improved. Then, when his mother was much better and it was safer to do so, Ben was able to talk about how angry he had felt, and this made more sense of his bad-tempered behaviour at school in contrast to his need to be good at home.

Reading is especially vulnerable to anxieties about growing up. There may also be a resistance to finding out, not wanting to know, as it were. Both of these may be linked to the wish to shut out problems at home. Alternatively the problems themselves may be too preoccupying to leave any space for work in the classroom.

Failure to read may also occur when a child cannot trust the teacher as an adult. Those who have learned to mistrust any authority, who cannot accept that the teacher knows more than they do, cannot readily make the relationship to the teacher which is so essential at this stage.

Philip needed a lot of help before he could read, yet he was an intelligent boy who enjoyed being taken around museums, and seemed to pick up a lot from such expeditions.

He very much wanted to be successful and clever, but could hardly bear to be taught. He was scornful and dismissive of the teachers, thought lessons were boring and, in spite of his efforts to learn on his own had scarcely begun to read by the time he was nearly eight.

This rejection was accompanied by a resentful relationship to his father. Philip had memories of a time when he was small and had a lot of fun with his father. He felt very let down when this all changed suddenly and father had to spend a lot of time working away from home. Philip was unprepared in advance and confused as to why it was necessary for his father to be away so much.

Rebecca showed her uncertainty about adult authority in a different way. She was thought to be very bright by her teacher but described as being so busy telling all the other children what to do that she never got round to her own reading book. This bossy little girl hated to admit that she could not do everything as well as her older sister, and even as a very small child wanted to do everything herself, with temper tantrums when she could not succeed. She was bright enough to succeed a lot of the time but she now had a habit of never listening to instructions properly and always being too impatient to wait to find out. In a way her potentially high level of intelligence was itself creating an obstacle to real work and achievement, combined as it was with an impatient and highly competitive spirit. Rebecca felt she had to know before she had been told. In this sense her intelligence was failing her.

Learning to read does indeed require assertiveness and a desire to master something. Ben, Philip and Rebecca all spent their assertiveness in a direction which left them without the achievement they sought. Controlling natural aggression and directing it into assertiveness is an important step towards learning.

This means there are problems not only for a child who is too aggressive, but also for one, like Charles, whose aggression had been so subdued that he was extremely passive. When games were introduced in the hope of making him more lively and competitive he appeared unable either to win or to lose. Both seemed equally dangerous. In the end he was encouraged to take a risk with board games of chance, where the threat was not too great, and when he could slowly become bolder.

Where direct help with reading did not work it is interesting to see how drawings, stories and games could help with the feelings that were making it difficult, and so make it easier to cope with the reading.

Perhaps, having looked at these children with reading problems, it is necessary to remember that there are, of course, times when trouble may arise because the teacher does not accept or understand the child. A cheerful, talkative child may be judged to be ahead and a shy one as behind, either may be pressed too hard, or the brave attempts of a child to struggle with a handicap may not be appreciated. Mismatch between teacher and child do not occur only as a problem in the child.

Whichever way it is we have come full circle, back to the relationship with the teacher, the hope for a good match between child and teacher, that we started with.

# Relations with other children in class

One way in which we learn to know ourselves better is in relation to others. What we started with our brothers and sisters is continued with our class mates. The comparisons with others are not only made by parents and teachers, but by the children themselves. It is a temptation to stimulate competition by making use of this tendency. This can encourage effort but it can also lead to attempts to copy the work of others, and so destroy a child's own originality and spontaneity.

The seven year old is beginning the process of identifying with a different kind of group from the family, and finding a place within it. There are advantages in being part of a group that stays together until a project is finished. The shared approval that comes from such co-operation is very rewarding.

Cheering your own class at the school sports is an example of this new kind of loyalty. Such loyalty means that some additional moralities have to be learned. "Telling tales" to teacher is not yet treated with quite so much scorn as it will be in a year or two, but seven year olds are already less likely to complain about each other to an adult.

Friendships have a firmer base as your seven year old develops an understanding of the claims and privileges these involve. Friends help to consolidate ideas about playing fairly and keeping to the rules, about sharing work and triumphs.

The sharpening of both competition and co-operation at this age are linked to those developments already stressed, a firmer sense of identity and a greater ability to understand the way that other people's minds work. The more secure children become in a sense of their own individuality, the more readily they can allow it to be submerged for a while, and to take pleasure in sharing what they have in common with others.

Seven year olds are still working towards this rather mature combination of rivalry and cooperation. In addition some will have a personality which inclines more to one or the other. In part this will be their own temperament and in part the result of the preferences at home, and their experiences with brothers and sisters. Occasionally a child will be at one extreme or the other but already many seven year olds do manage, at least some of the time, to shift from competition to loyal sharing with remarkable maturity. If this sometimes breaks down we should not be too surprised.

The ability to be part of your class group is required over and over again during the school day, in work and in the school playground. From this classroom group will also come the ever widening circle of friends that the seven year old draws on outside school. The influence of these new loyalties and social skills will be felt in a great deal of play and leisure activities, and to these we will return in the next chapter.

# Reluctance to go to school

Both home and school are involved in the problem of the child who begins to resist going to school. It is of concern to both as a source of stress and anxiety, and causes much distress to parents and teachers and, above all, to the children themselves.

It is often only when reluctance to go to school becomes refusal that real concern is expressed and some action is taken. With hindsight it is possible to see warning signs before a last straw led to the final breakdown.

It is not easy to make a list of possible causes when the anxiety about school is usually part of a web of circumstances and feelings, in which the child's part may be very difficult to untangle. There is also therefore no one "cure" for all occasions.

These are some of the issues that have been found to be connected with reluctance or refusal to go to school: a boy with a partial hearing loss which had not been discovered; a mother who was finding it almost unbearable to see the last of her five babies going off for most of the day; a boy who had picked up fears that something would happen to his mother while he was away, and another girl who refused to go back to school after being home with a broken leg, when she had gained a lot of attention and sympathy.

Even these reasons are not really a sufficient explanation since many other children still manage to go to school in spite of similar things happening to them or their family. Indeed, for some children with troubled homes, the reliability and orderliness of school can provide some respite.

It is also not good enough to blame parents – mothers are especially vulnerable to being criticised. The adjustment required in order to settle at school from the child's point of view has probably been emphasised enough in this chapter, yet neither can we blame the schools as a matter of course. After all most children do make that adjustment, without too much pain or anxiety.

The boy, Brian, who had some hearing loss was certainly caught up in the blame that was passed around. "It should never have happened", "why didn't the teacher (the doctor, the school nurse, his mother) notice something". Somehow Brian had slipped through the net and the mutual blaming was one way of relieving the guilty feelings of those involved. This did little to help Brian who had lost confidence; unaware of what was happening to him he felt he was stupid because he could not understand. As well as a hearing-aid he needed help to rebuild his confidence.

Lindy's mother who was only too ready to accept the excuses Lindy found to stay home, had no deliberate intention to deprive her of school. She was horrified when the occasional excuses became more and more frequent and she was visited by the school's social worker. It was only at this point that Lindy's father became concerned and his greater involvement in the family that this caused, provided a turning point, not just in getting Lindy to school, but in the support his wife needed so much.

There are many other instances when gaining the interest of father and including him in the plans has turned out to be crucial and a great relief to everybody, including their child.

When Emma's broken leg was healed her mother listened to her worries and showed some sympathy for the difficulties she would have in catching up with her class. Her own confidence that Emma would return nevertheless was important in avoiding the sympathy becoming collusion. There would inevitably be some problems for Emma in getting back, even though her teacher had been very helpful in sending work home for her to do.

Most children will have some occasions when they are unwilling to go to school for some reason or another. Books about schooldays are full of examples. Not every bit of reluctance is a danger signal for future school refusal, but listening to your child's worries, trying to sort out potential problems early on, linked with your own certainty, as a parent, that going to school is the best thing to do, even if it isn't perfect, can avoid the problem getting bigger.

The children themselves may complain about problems at school, maybe with an individual teacher or bullying from other children. When Keith told his mother about a boy who made threats to try to get things from him, she asked him what he would prefer. Should she go and talk to the teacher as she had done in earlier years, over other worries? Keith did not want her to do this as it would make him look babyish.

Nor did he like the alternative of going to the teacher himself. After talking it over Keith was encouraged to face up to a confrontation with the boy, which he had been avoiding. The conversation with his mother had also provided a useful opportunity to help him with a difficult moment in the process of growing up by facing him directly with his feelings about remaining too dependent upon his mother.

Sometimes children show anxieties about changing for P.E. or games. Dealing with these sympathetically may also avoid resistance to school spilling over into complete refusal. Once the pattern of not going to school is established it becomes very hard to break. So there needs to be an emphasis on getting a child back to school immediately, with whatever special arrangements make it tolerable.

Even where the main fault is felt to lie with the school careful thought needs to be given before changing schools is taken to be the answer. In many cases some other problem quickly follows the transfer to the new school. Where, all the same, it does seem necessary, a carefully managed changeover, with time to say some appropriate goodbyes will be important.

Truanting, without their parents' knowing, is unusual for children at this age. This offers some support for the idea that it is rarely a matter simply of avoiding school. The ultimate cause can sometimes lie a long way back, in some more or less forgotten incident, an early hospital stay, or threats to leave made during a crisis between the parental partners. If the problem is really severe then some outside help, in the form of family or individual therapy, may need to be called upon.

Whatever the cause, if any child refuses to go to school it is always a major test of the co-operation between family and school.

CHAPTER FOUR

# PLAY AND IMAGINATION

## Solitary play

An enormous amount of your seven year old's play is likely to be with other children and it may seem that playing alone is never a matter of choice. Still, there are times for most children when they like to be by themselves, when they can set aside the need to consult others or fit in with them. Such times are most likely to be when they are indoors, making models, drawing and colouring, sewing or handling technical equipment, all of which make use of the considerable manual skills that seven year olds now have.

This is indeed an age when so many skills and interests are developing that many things may be taken up with apparent enthusiasm, only to be left still incomplete. It is also an age when children become critical of their own efforts, find how difficult it is to make their drawing or model look like the real thing and so discouragement can set in. There is a limit to how much a child should be pressed to finish something before beginning anything new. It is much more important not to allow such discouragement to dampen all creative efforts.

Hobbies and collections are equally susceptible to being all absorbing for a time and then dropped. Something may have been learned in the process, but any educational aspect is not the real source of the pleasure for the child. The collecting is the thing. Emphasis upon turning it into a serious study of the materials involved may just result in boredom, once again killing spontaneity and creativity. The items collected may in themselves seem not much better than junk to the parents, tickets and labels for instance, so it is not the value either which is the essential factor.

Collecting, like the ownership of toys, has a part to play in confirming your own identity. The ferocity with which such property rights can be defended, against siblings and others, illustrates the strength of feelings about ownership. Once ownership is secure however the same child who fought to keep what was theirs may be generous and sharing, and part of the pleasure in collecting often lies in the possibilities for comparing and making swaps with other children.

This is typical seven year old behaviour. Pride in ownership is not necessarily related to size and value, as many parents have found to their disappointment after some special present has been purchased. "I spent such a lot on it, and he never plays with it" is, alas, a common complaint.

Whilst there is some link between play and school-based activities, and reading is an obvious example, on the whole children will expect home to be a place where they relax from the rigours of school and formal learning. For many of them, much of the time, that will mean watching television, listening to pop music cassettes and playing with video games.

For the lonely or shy child these may become a replacement for playing with other children, but in many homes they are not specifically solitary. Even if a child watches, listens or plays alone, these activities are likely to provide the basis for discussing and arguing with friends or family. It is time to move on to that play with other children briefly mentioned earlier.

## Playing with others

The range of the seven year old's play is now greatly widened by the addition of all sorts of games, with rules and procedures which were beyond the scope of younger children. Such games can make use of new abilities in counting and reading, plus all sorts of qualities of understanding, awareness and tolerance, all of which have been discussed before as part of the seven year old's gradual development.

Only children may have to make extra efforts to fit in with these more demanding group games. Earlier experience of mixing with children outside school will have provided a useful background, but it can still be quite hard to make up for the intensity of the relationship that exists between children of the same family.

Various attempts may be made to make the group situation more manageable. For instance, two girls who were both only children had a best friend from whom they were inseparable. Betty found one who was older who tended to look after her, and Maggie's friend was younger, someone with whom she could be boss. Both seemed to be trying to make up for something.

When we watch children on holiday, on the beach say, we can observe how readily they seem to make friends, particularly with others who are about their own age. Longer term friendships are not so easy to maintain though and that can be a real source of heartache at this age. Laura got on well enough with other children but she had one best friend with whom she always played. When this friend moved away to another area she was really distressed; it was unusual for her to need so much encouragement to go out to play. On the other hand Tom seems to play happily with whatever group of children he is with and does not make special friends. Both, of course, are "normal" children. There is no absolutely normal pattern of friendships, only a need for some relationships with a reasonable amount of give and take.

Friendly play with parents deserves a special mention. Only children may especially involve parents, for instance in playing board games, but it can be an enlightening experience for all children, even in much bigger families. There is a special satisfaction in being able to beat parents and other adults in this safe way. The feelings of excitement are evidence enough of the reality of the competition. The fact that at the end nobody is actually destroyed makes these games a very useful way of learning to cope with strong feelings about winning and losing. An additional value of playing with parents is provided by their example in winning and losing with good grace.

Most play however will be with the new circle of friends being made, principally through school of course. How much vigorous play can take place indoors will depend on how much space there is and on the rules of the house. The amount of active play that could be managed indoors with under fives is no longer possible, but games like hide and seek and hunt the thimble are usually tolerable.

An important part of making friends is in the opportunities they might provide for visiting, giving your child the chance to see homes with other customs, and so continuing the useful process of comparison and widening of experience which the seven year old is engaged in.

Out of doors the possibility of using large equipment has a special place in building confidence, and there is relief in giving full vent to pent up energy. Of course, group games, whether indoors or outdoors, call on your seven year old's resources in managing competition. Team games make extra demands in terms of cooperation, it means sinking some of your own interests for the benefit of the team as a whole. It is a lot to ask of your seven year old who is having to hold on to a sense of individual identity which is still a bit wobbly.

At school or on holiday when there is an adult around the rules may be kept for quite a time. But outdoors, where play is anyway more physical, it is not surprising when such games end in a more primitive rough and tumble.

Play is for pleasure and, on the one hand, it flourishes when there is freedom from lots of restrictions and demands. On the other hand the seven year old still needs surroundings which are familiar enough, and where there is a framework which offers a reasonable degree of reassurance for play to be really free and spontaneous. The satisfactions to be obtained are potentially great, and the chance to exercise imagination a way of enriching life, both now and later. Play is fun, but it is not trivial. For any child life without play is limited and impoverished.

# Imagination

Why is the exercise of imagination in play so important? What does it involve and imply? The ability to pretend is something that has evolved throughout childhood. It means that your child has an understanding of things that are not immediately observable, knows what is real and what is not. Taken for granted in your seven year old, it is worth stopping to take in the immensity of the step in thinking that this represents.

Do you remember the shared delight in the games of make-believe played by your children at an earlier age? How you were invited to join in and pretend to drink from a toy cup, for example? We had understood the game and, in a way, solved a puzzle they had set us, and that seemed to be immensely satisfying. This kind of "let's pretend" play is an early step in separating out reality and imagination, and using it for fun.

Your seven year old may use their imagination in their drawing and painting and introduce fantasy into play with dolls or models. They may be more self-conscious about being caught talking to themselves and keep this play more private. Perhaps this is partly because parents get anxious about children "living in a world of their own".

It may also be a part of a more general worry parents have about the need for children at this age to know the difference between fact and fiction. Parents need to know, for very practical reasons, whether their children are telling the truth. Maybe this sometimes gets caught up in a discouragement of what is seen as just being fanciful.

In any case this is a time when there is likely to be some sharing of pretend play with other children. We saw that Laura and Tom, with whom we began this book, have moved a long way since early childhood, in understanding the real world. They also understand other people in a more complete way. They now expect that others will be able to understand what they are doing when they make up an imaginary world. Their games of make believe now take on a new form.

Laura will ask her friends to take parts in her imaginary world, as she did when she was at nursery school, but now she is prepared to accommodate their imagination also. Their combined flights of fancy may take them far away or the play may be made from everyday observation at home and school, but the fact that it is "pretend" is never in real doubt. However this play-acting does involve real feelings and may still be a way of working something out about emotions which come originally from the world of reality.

The experience of allowing another person's world to influence your own, opening yourself up as it were, is not only a basis for more friendly play. It also makes other communication possible, and so creates a foundation for learning.

These uses of imagination are reminders that the world is not only made up of what is true and what is false. Playful fantasy can also turn into comedy, and your seven year old may well try out a newly discovered sense of humour. April fool jokes, riddles, tricks and jokes with words are all immensely popular. Children's earlier belief in magic has weakened, although superstitions often flourish, especially when they have a playful element. This playing with the reality of the world does seem to have a very useful function, allowing children to come to terms with this reality in a kinder way than would be possible without it.

Fantasy companions have usually disappeared by now, but fantasy has not. It may be explained away as dream-like but it remains a useful way of creating a world that can be controlled. More than that, it is a way of extending an understanding of what is possible, providing an experience of letting your mind roam freely and invent. Such capacities to invent and to go beyond the immediate are among the greatest glories of human achievement.

CHAPTER FIVE

# SOME THOUGHTS ON PARENTING

The emphasis of this book has been on your child and the intention has been to focus on understanding rather than on advice. The developments that have been described will, we hope, support all those involved with seven year olds in their understanding of what expectations are appropriate.

In any case the wide range, from one child to another, in school achievements; in the drive to be independent; in sociability; in verbal skills and in numerous other aspects of personality, mean that it is not possible to define a single set of rules about helping a seven year old to grow up well and happy.

Instead the advice given, if you can call it that, is that by observing, listening and talking to your children, under-standing will increase and your children be more interesting, enjoyable and maybe even more amenable. Talking to them will also have the advantage of increasing their ability in language, in a way that no amount of chatting with their friends can do.

Growing up well and happy may be the aim we have for our children, but we have to accept that complete happiness is not possible. There are bound to be sad times and it would seem odd to have a child who could not share sad feelings sometimes. As your seven year old is more able to understand, and care about, the opinions and feelings of other people so those opinions will influence their own. Allowing feelings to show is more acceptable for boys, as well as girls, than it once was. A child afraid or ashamed of feelings might in the end manage not to see the sadness or hurt of others.

# A life of your own

Parents still carry a 24 hour a day responsibility, although their seven year old now spends so much time at school or with friends. Even if there are no other children at home who are younger and still very dependent, there are quite enough worries about what your seven year old is up to, how he is being judged by others, whether he is safe on his way home, is she behaving herself at the party, does she get on with her new teacher?

Yet seven year olds themselves benefit when parents, mothers as well as fathers, have some life of their own. Some respite from a parent's intense preoccupation with their children leaves both sides a bit freer to be themselves. Many mothers, especially those bringing up children on their own, report how much they miss adult company. A job outside the home might help, yet might still not meet the need for a more intimate, confidential friendship.

One of the advantages of having a child at school is that it increases the opportunities for meeting other parents and it is easy to see that getting involved in school functions, helping out at the fete, or accompanying a school outing, is welcomed by some parents. Others, may, less willingly, get pressed into service by their children.

Whatever the means by which you have a life of your own: work outside the home; a close friend in whom to confide; involvement in projects at school or elsewhere; outings with your partner; it seems necessary to have some time away from parenting.

## Adjustment and crises

Adjustment is sometimes talked about as though it were a permanent state that a child should always be in. Such complete adjustment is no more possible than complete happiness. It is rather a process of adapting to each change or new challenge with more or less success. If the successful occasions outnumber the failures then we do indeed have a normally well-adjusted child.

In a way each new demand on your child is a kind of crisis. There are moments, in development for instance, when a change is demanded. They are bound to happen as a normal part of growing up. Some, like starting school, are almost inevitable in our society, others are quite likely to happen, such as the arrival of a new baby.

These are events which can be anticipated to a large extent and the change that is required can be managed without too much discomfort. A "real crisis" is usually associated with something unexpected and unpleasant: a parent or child going into hospital; the illness or death of a close relative or friend; losing your job; some local disaster. All require some readjustment of your life. With support to find the strength to rise to a crisis you may even find your capacity to cope is improved.

Helping your seven year old to manage the crises in his or her life may mean that they come out of it with a better way of coping with future problems. It is easy to underestimate the demands for major change that are made on a child. Some may be dismissed as being a natural part of growing up, or as something "they are too young to understand".

A child's experience of coming through a crisis safely will help to give confidence when the next one is faced. It is a time, of course, when the primary importance of the family becomes clear, with home as the place where feelings can be expressed, and the value of trusted and loving parents becomes paramount.

# Family history

One of the things that parents do, most of the time without thinking about it, is the holding of family history. This includes your seven year old's personal history, who picks up the comments you make and remembers them, without necessarily intending to do so.

Children do ask questions about their past, of course, and there are times when the family snapshots or other records are taken out and shared, and these activities reinforce the sense of a particular family and where they belong within it.

There is a more casual way, however, in which that sense of belonging is constantly reinforced. The girl watching her baby brother being breast fed and being told "you were fed just the same way when you were a baby"; the boy being encouraged to turn out his toy box and relinquish some old toys, deciding to keep the one that was the very first toy grandma gave him; being reminded "that's the nursery school you used to go to"; mother sharing a letter and saying "your aunt Jane who went to Canada a long time ago, is coming to visit us".

The examples could be endless, their function a very useful one. Apart from their setting down of personal history, they provide a model of how events can be put into a framework, and so make more sense. The more they can make sense of their own life, the more your seven year olds can feel it is manageable.

## Your 7 year old's view of adult life

At the other extreme of holding the family history, parents also have a view of the future which they pass on to their children in a similar, casual way. Comments about "what the world is coming to" are heard by a child and more or less understood.

The seven year old's major preoccupation with the future, however, is likely to be at a more personal level. What view might they have of what it is like to be grown up? This will no longer be based entirely on their parent's way of life, important though that is. Children are constantly observing and trying to understand the world around them.

There are, though, two aspects of adult life which are of special interest, yet cannot, indeed generally should not, be understood from their first hand experience. We do not involve children in intimate sexual relationships, nor do we expect them to take full time jobs. Indeed, there are laws to prevent either of these happening. Children do, of course, have ideas about sex and work, but these are based on limited observation, whether in real life or in the TV they watch, and on the comments and attitudes of the adults around them.

Your seven year old still has difficulty handling abstract ideas, and this will place a further limitation on understanding. Some reference has already been made in an earlier chapter to the continuing curiosity about sex, even though this may be less openly expressed. Enough has probably been said about the need for information about sex to be honest, but within a child's ability to understand, in order to avoid a view, distorted by false ideas and evasions, which might colour their attitudes for many years.

Not many seven year old's will be able to give a reasoned answer to the question "what do you want to be (or do) when you grow up?" Their description of any job tends to be based upon what they can see in a very concrete way. What they can see may be a more or less trivial aspect of the real job.

So a policeman may be described as someone who rides about in a car, stops cars that are going too fast and so on. These are ideas based upon actual observation. Others may be based on less direct experience, such as "they catch people who have committed crimes", or words to that effect. But a really inclusive idea, such as "maintaining law and order" is unlikely to be produced. The words may be known, but the idea is still too abstract for most seven year olds.

Their notion of what various jobs are worth will probably be equally limited. It may, therefore, seem much harder to be a bus driver than a teacher, on the basis that a teacher only has to talk all day.

Driving, in one form or another, still seems to be an important ambition for many children, even if it is no longer in the old tradition of every boys' wish to be an engine driver. Being in charge of a powerful machine must be especially attractive when you are still coming to terms with control of your own body and of strong feelings. It must also feel like a short cut to sharing the same power and strength as an adult.

It is possible that some other ambitions, for instance to be a doctor or a nurse, come from a desire to look after other people, based on an idea of mothering that has been gathered at first hand. So it is not surprising that these have traditionally been early ambitions, especially for girls. As with the driver ambition, they also convey a sense of getting on equal terms with an adult, and especially with the most important adults in your life.

Many of the ideas about grown ups' work that seven year olds have are amusing and delightful, but they are also part of the whole struggle to grow up. We hope this book has conveyed some of the delights and difficulties of this struggle.

# FURTHER READING

*On Learning to Read: the child's fascination with meaning*, Bruno Bettelheim, Thames & Hudson, London, 1982
*Children's Minds*, Margaret Donaldson, Fontana, 1978
*Parenting Threads: caring for children when couples part*, National Stepfamily Association, 1992
*The Emotional Experience of Learning and Teaching*, Isca Salzberger-Wittenberg, Gianna Henry & Elsie Osborne, Routledge & Kegan Paul, London, 1983

# HELPFUL ORGANISATIONS

Exploring Parenthood, Latimer Education Centre, 194 Freston Road, London W10 6TT. (National Advice Line for parents: 081-960-1678, 10.00 – 4.0 p.m. Monday to Friday)

National Stepfamily Association, 72 Willesden Lane, London NW6 7TA. (071-372-0844)

National Children's Bureau, 8 Wakley Street, London, EC1V 7QW.

Advisory Centre for Education, 18 Victoria Park Square, London, E2 9PB. (081-980-4596)

# UNDERSTANDING YOUR CHILD

## ORDER FORM FOR TITLES IN THIS SERIES

Send to:  Rosendale Press Ltd., 8 Ponsonby Place,
London SW1 4PT

*Price per volume:* £7.99 inc. post & packing

| | |
|---|---|
| Understanding Your Baby by Lisa Miller | . . . . . copies |
| Understanding Your 1 Year Old by Deborah Steiner | . . . . . copies |
| Understanding Your 2 Year Old by Susan Reid | . . . . . copies |
| Understanding Your 3 Year Old by Judith Trowell | . . . . . copies |
| Understanding Your 4 Year Old by Lisa Miller | . . . . . copies |
| Understanding Your 5 Year Old by Lesley Holditch | . . . . . copies |
| Understanding Your 6 Year Old by Deborah Steiner | . . . . . copies |
| Understanding Your 7 Year Old by Elsie Osborne | . . . . . copies |
| Understanding Your 8 Year Old by Lisa Miller | . . . . . copies |
| Understanding Your 9 Year Old by Dora Lush | . . . . . copies |
| Understanding Your 10 Year Old by Jonathan Bradley | . . . . . copies |
| Understanding Your 11 Year Old by Eileen Orford | . . . . . copies |
| Understanding Your Handicapped Child by Valerie Sinason | . . . . . copies |
| Understanding 12–14 Year Olds by Margot Waddell | . . . . . copies |
| Understanding 15–17 Year Olds<br>     by Hélène Dubinsky & Jonathan Bradley | . . . . . copies |
| Understanding 18–20 Year Olds<br>     by Gianna Williams & Beta Copley | . . . . . copies |

Total amount enclosed: £. . . . . . . . . . .

Name . . . . . . . . . . . . . . . . . . . . . . . . . . . .

Address . . . . . . . . . . . . . . . . . . . . . . . . . . . .

. . . . . . . . . . . . . . . . . . . Post code . . . . . . . . . . . . . . . . . . .